AF576813

Dana Hoey: Experiments in Primitive Living

University of Maryland Baltimore County

Distributed Art Publishers

2010

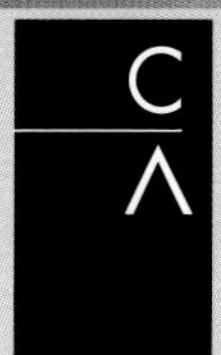

Center for Art Design and Visual Culture

Dana Hoey: Experiments in Primitive Living

Maurice Berger

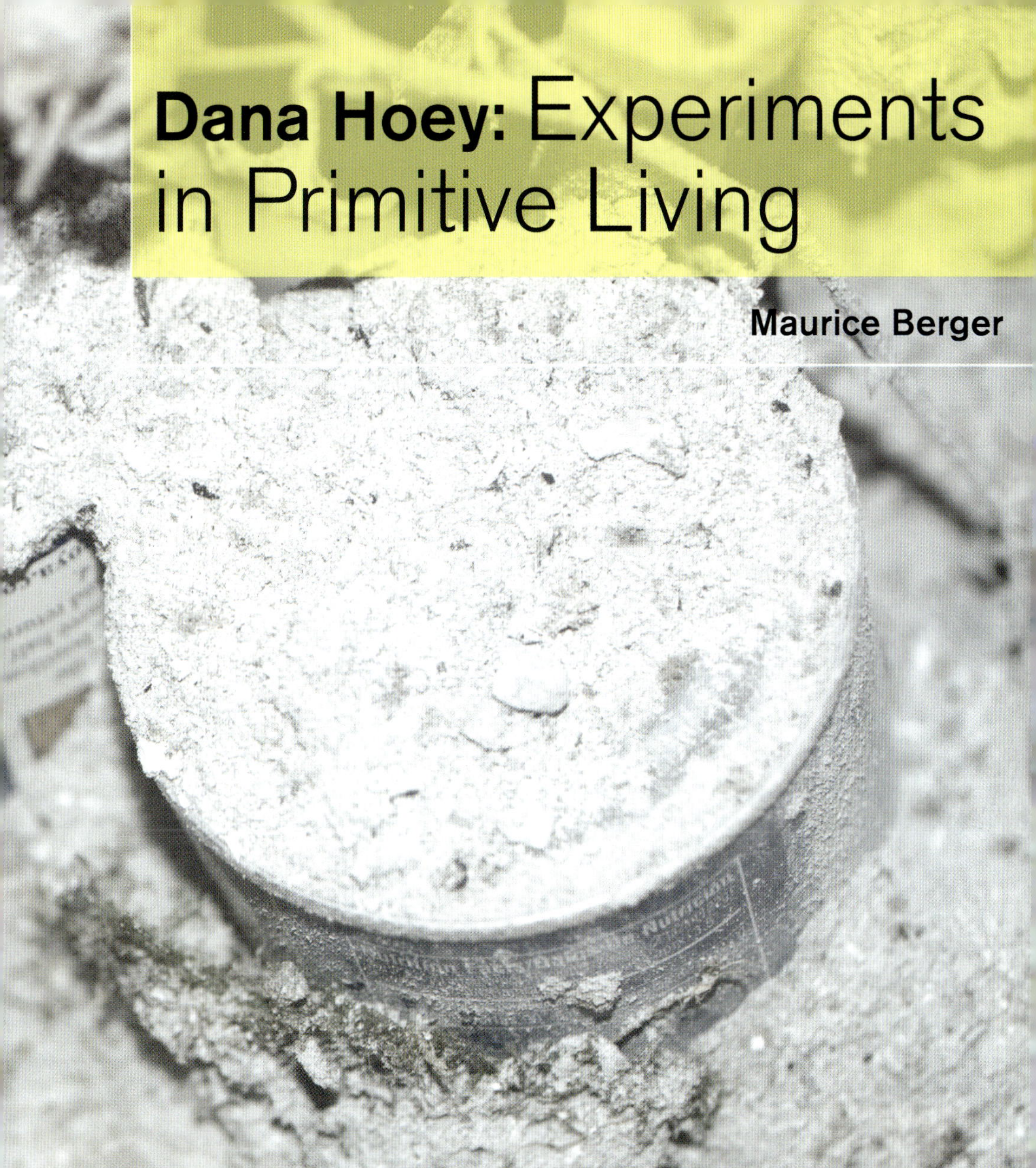

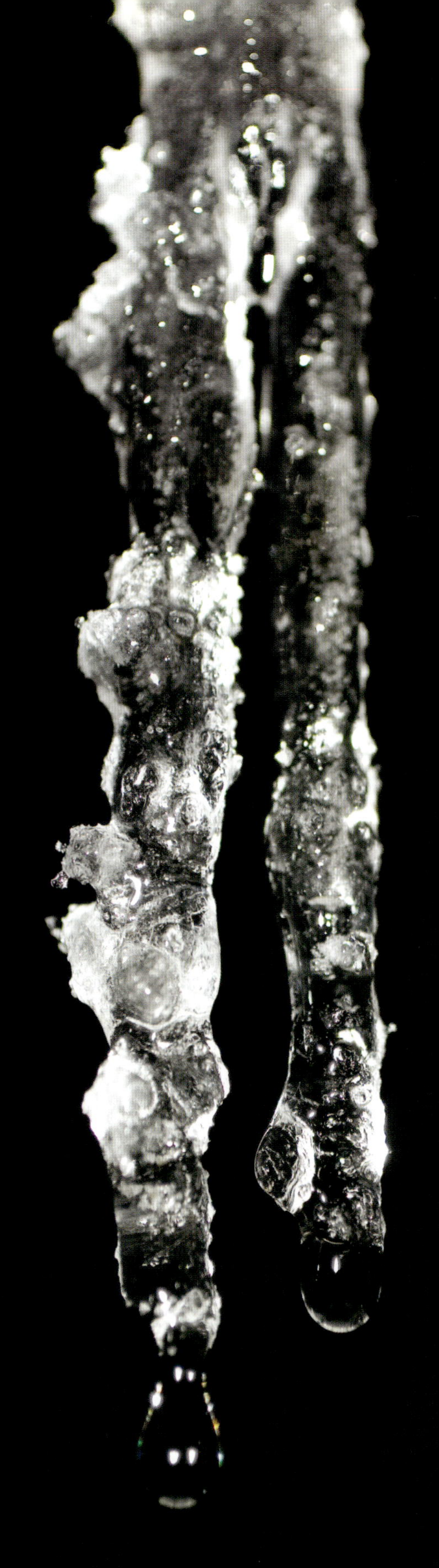

Insects, old women, and plastic tools are the inhabitants of a potential world. *Experiments in Primitive Living* is a cycle of photographs that imagine what the world would be like under five different weather conditions—ash, freeze, thaw, flood, and drought. It is a deliberately nonhierarchical archive of different photographic styles: product shot, scientific photo, portrait, and epic narrative. Because the subjects in the pictures are also on equal ground—for example, the spore and the face merit the same size and resolution—old categories serve not as aesthetic end-games but as an homage to the camera's ability to inform, to sell, to turn you on, or to tell a story. In this possible world, there is a power vacuum, an absence of infrastructure, and now the overlooked have stepped in. Old women may rule, silently. The small detail may outlast the large story. The icicle may outlive the guitar player.

Dana Hoey

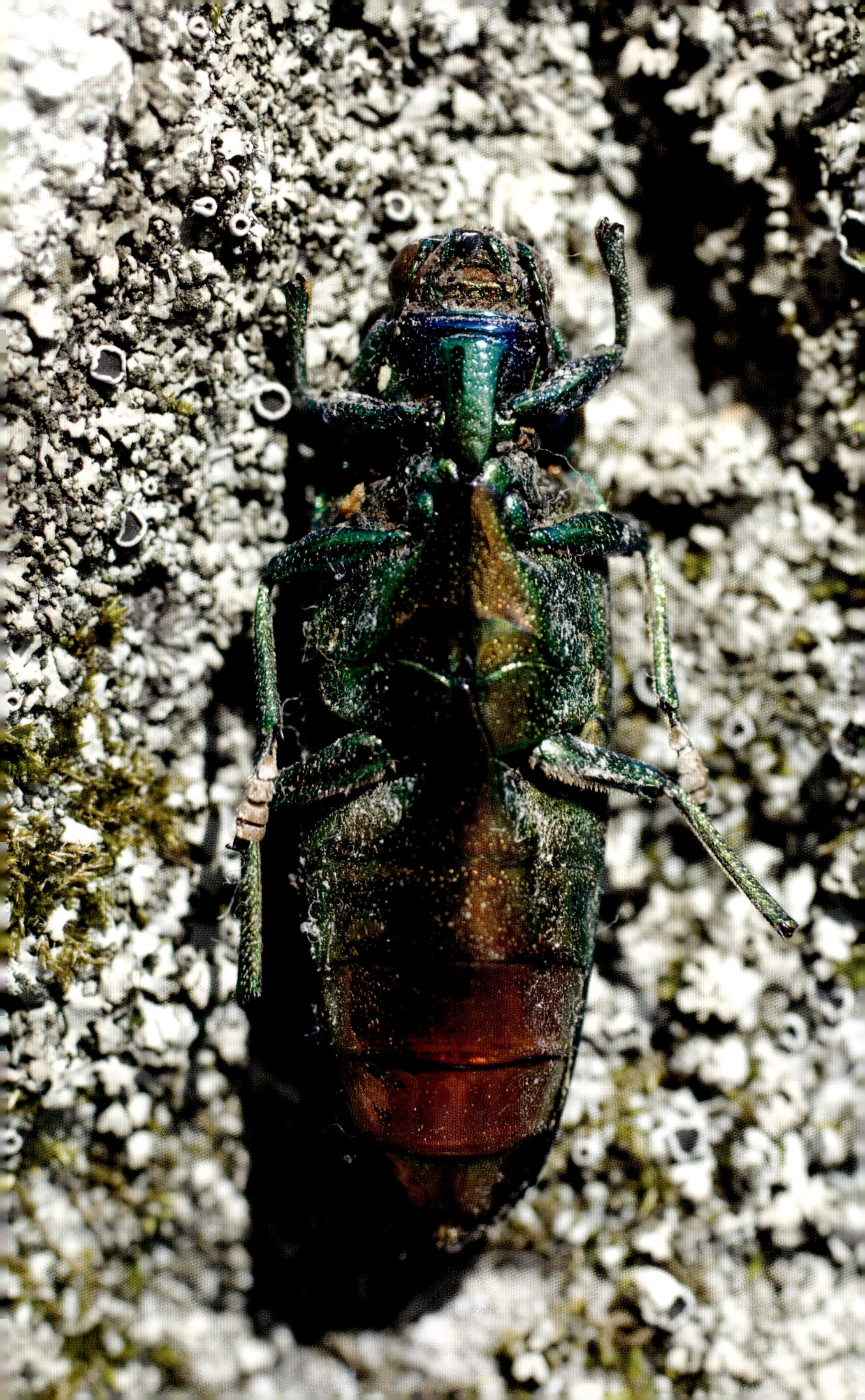

Silent Spring

Maurice Berger

Nearly a half-century ago, the marine biologist and nature writer Rachel Carson published a book that would spawn a modern ecological movement: *Silent Spring*. The work, about the disastrous consequences of the unlimited use of pesticides, is at once a journalistic account, a scientific tract, and a cautionary tale. Carson cites scientific studies on the dangers to wildlife and humans from exposure to pesticides. She recounts in painstaking detail the stories of cities and towns where the deployment of pesticides, such as DDT, had destroyed wildlife and sickened and killed humans. She argues that nothing less than a nationwide ban on DDT and other harmful insecticides would be necessary to avoid environmental catastrophe.

Carson's treatise begins on a fictional note, with "A Fable for Tomorrow." She describes a once idyllic town—much like the place of her childhood, Springdale, Pennsylvania—a vision of a people in harmony with nature, where fauna and flora thrive in abundance. The tranquil turned frightening as a "strange blight crept over the area and everything began to change."[1] Plants and animals perished. People became ill and many died. A hush fell over the town, an image driven by the abiding metaphor of Carson's epochal book: silence. "It was spring without voices. On the mornings that once throbbed with the dawn chorus of robins, catbirds, doves, jays, wrens, and scores of other bird voices, there was no sound; only silence lay over the fields and woods and marsh."[2]

Carson's metaphor of silence works on multiple levels. It evokes the stillness of death, when the sounds of nature—the rush of leafy branches swept by wind, the song of birds, the utterances of man—cease to exist. It brings to mind the numbed silence, the literal inability to speak, engendered by the terror that would no doubt arise in the wake of such a catastrophe.

It suggests the difficulty of imposing a neat, lucid narrative on a scene of horrifying devastation. Carson's recounting of ecological upheaval is less a story, a continuum of events recited in chronological order, than a patchwork of unsettling details. It is as if words and logic are no longer useful in our attempt to grasp the enormity and the staggering repercussions of the calamity she describes.

Perhaps more than any other artwork of the past half-century, Dana Hoey's *Experiments in Primitive Living* (2008), in its aesthetic, conceptual, and social ambitions, embodies Carson's allegory of silence. Hoey represents the successive phases of an unnamed, imaginary ecological disaster—her version of a "spring without voices"—not with words, but through vivid color photographs. *Experiments'* five sections, *Ash, Freeze, Thaw, Drought*, and *Flood*, consist of salon-style arrangements of up to ten images of varying dimensions. The pictures do not tell a coherent story. Rather, they depict a range of phenomena and situations, from extremely close-up details to nearly panoramic landscapes, that relate to each other obliquely or tangentially. Their stylistic diversity—appropriating as they do the look of commercial product shots, film stills, or scientific, documentary, or portrait photographs—enhances the project's mood of ambiguity and dislocation.

In *Ash*, a large, opalescent insect clings to an ash-covered plastic leaf (*Green Bug*, 2007); strands of a gray wig fall over pale skin (*The Police*, 2008); and a young woman stares into space, dumbstruck. In *Freeze*, the needles of thirteen identical compasses, possibly damaged by the extreme cold, point in different directions; two icicles glisten against a stark black background (*Icicles*, 2008); and a nude, ice-covered body lies in a desolate field. In *Thaw*, a parasitic fungus grows on the trunk of a tree (*Maple Fungus*, 2008); a red seedling emerges from the damp ground; and bright orange newts slither in a pile. *Flood* consists of two solitary pictures: a large-scale photograph of rippling water (*Flood*, 2008) and, in what may well be the project's most poignant image, a life-size shot of an emergency radio. (*Radio*, 2008). In *Drought*, a primitive device set into parched soil collects water from the atmosphere (*Solar Still*, 2008); a large, desiccated leaf rests on the hood of a car (*Canna*, 2008);

and legs straddle a surreptitious campfire buried in the ground in order to avoid detection.

Hoey's imagery is bold, evocative, but also inscrutable and unexpected. Traditional hierarchies of size and scale are inverted or distorted. The minutiae of nature—an icicle, a leaf, an insect—command equal or greater visual space than humans. A tiny seedling looms large; a child is dwarfed by a vast landscape. Expectations are reversed. Young people are depicted as weak, stunned, and overwhelmed; elderly women read as strong and confident. The line between life and death, animate and inanimate, is blurred: an ice-sheathed body may be a corpse or numbed by hypothermia. The limbs of a woman appear metallic: are they human or do they belong to a doll, a robot, or a mannequin?

The structure of the work further undercuts narrative coherence. Because the five sections of *Experiments* are deployed within the spare, gray-washed sectors of a cruciform arrangement of walls, they must be viewed episodically and cannot be seen at once in totality. As the viewer moves through its discrete sections, the work invites discovery, offering visual surprises and erratic juxtapositions and vistas. Owing much to the phenomenological games of minimalist sculpture of the 1960s—in which viewers comprehend the shapes and dimensions of large-scale abstract monoliths only by moving through and around them—the journey through the piece forces us to stay in the moment and take nothing for granted, much like the stranded survivors it presents.

The imagery of *Experiments* oscillates between dispassionate, keenly observed depictions of the physical effects of environmental catastrophe and the human reaction to these events—bodies scarred by trauma, rendered speechless by fear, and driven by the will to survive. It represents a world scorched, frozen, or flooded almost beyond livability, a post-apocalyptic landscape where basic, life-giving resources are either unavailable or scarce. As the French philosopher Jean-François Lyotard observes in a litany of circumstances that could easily apply to *Experiments*, terror is the inevitable psychological response to such extreme states of deprivation: "privation of light, terror of darkness; privation of others, terror of solitude; privation of language, terror of silence; privation of objects, terror of emptiness; privation of life, terror of death."[3]

As if to parallel the dispossession it depicts, *Experiments'* isolated and disjointed content and organization deprive the viewer of the lucid—and reassuring—narratives associated with photographic storytelling. By confusing viewers, and hence making them uncomfortable, the work allows them momentarily, if abstractly, to identify with the de-centered psychological states it represents. "I so wanted to do away with traditional photographic narratives," says Hoey, "that I made collages in the period leading up to *Experiments* that completely banished the possibility of telling a story."[4] The resulting series, *Pattern Recognition*, consists of rhythmic, kaleidoscopic arrangements of photographic fragments *(River of Time*, 2006). Juxtaposing facets of various types of imagery—the female nude, for example, with the classical portrait—the works' opaque, abstract surfaces resist the spatial illusionism, direct correspondence to reality, and narrative clarity of conventional photography.

***Experiments'* rejection of** narrative unity—an abiding characteristic of the artist's work in general—is meant as a political act, one grounded in the ideologies of environmentalism and feminism. The imperative to explain the natural world through tidy and predictable stories is, of course, another way of controlling it. The need to assert our authority over nature, exemplified by this analytical impulse "was conceived in arrogance, born in the Neanderthal Age of biology and philosophy, when it was supposed that nature exists for the convenience of man," notes Rachel Carson.[5]

In the savage and desolate world of *Experiments in Primitive Living*, man is at risk of being destroyed by the very nature he has mistreated and plundered. The hapless, terror-stricken souls represented there are beyond the point where language and culture can save them or even afford them dominance or superiority over the natural world. "These people are falling silent, they are literally dumbstruck, because they are no longer able to control their environment," observes the artist. "In a terrifying situation like this, language literally fails: the human instinct is to slink around, observe, physically react, but not talk."[6]

Hoey's environmental activism informs an earlier literary collaboration with the biographer and social critic Gretchen Rubin: *Profane Waste* (2006).[7] The book, a series of full-page color photographs punctuated by short analytical texts, muses on the absurdity of economic and material excess, the kind of

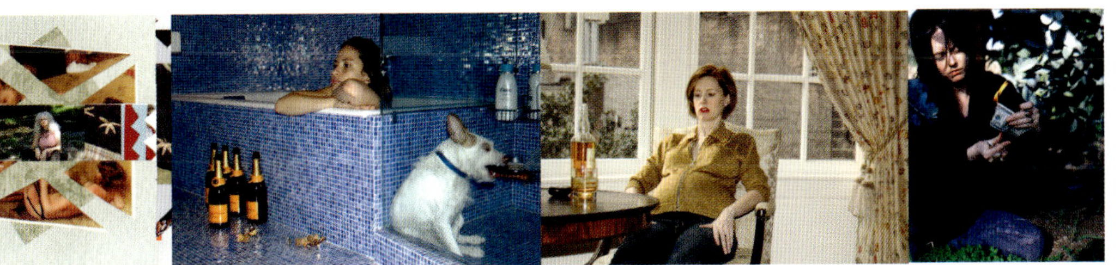

irresponsible behavior that would, a year later, lead to the direst global economic crisis since the Great Depression. Its uncanny, somewhat improbable images serve as allegories of reckless consumption: pregnant women smoke cigarettes (*Pregnant Smoker 2*, 2001) or down shots of Scotch (*Dewar's Mother*, 2005); a woman burns a real hundred-dollar bill (*Profane Waste*, 2001); another bathes in expensive wine (*Champagne Bath, 2005*).

This imagery speaks to an irrational, and all too real contradiction in human nature: that between the craving for financial and material reward and the compulsion to waste, even at the expense of further economic gain. *Profane Waste* represents the calm before the metaphoric storm of *Experiments in Primitive Living*. "The only way to keep . . . control over an object forever is to destroy it," writes Rubin in an aphorism that underscores the extent to which both projects focus on the human will to assert superiority over the world.[8] Unlike the terror-stricken inhabitants of the latter work, however, the characters of the former are spared the reality of the limitations of this control as well as its potentially catastrophic effects.

Hoey's ecological statements are not just cautionary tales about pending disaster; they are also feminist meditations on the role of men in destroying the earth and the capability of women to save it. One of the abiding symbols of *Experiments* is that of the older woman as icon of silent strength. The gray-haired grandmothers who stoically assess dangerous situations (*Thaw: Mrs. Jacoby*, 2005) are the project's most fearless and stable characters. Their silence, unlike that of their youthful contemporaries, is not a sign of fear or weakness; rather it is an outward manifestation of the intense concentration, inner peace, and quiet observation necessary to guide a terrified population to safety.

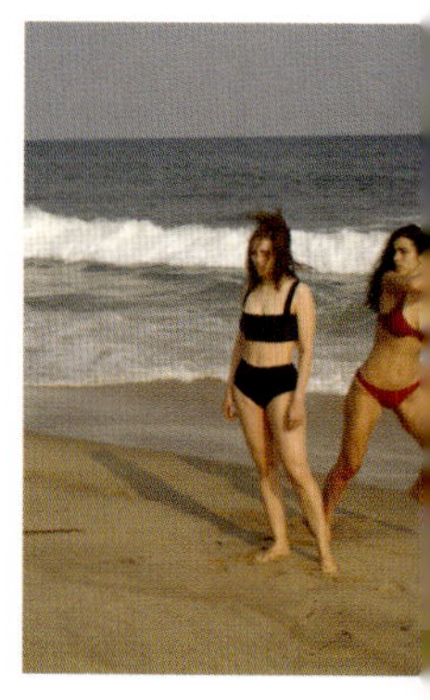

Women have long been the subjects of Hoey's work. For the past twenty years, she has relentlessly explored their relationship to power, male authority, sexuality, and self-image, predominantly through *faux verité* shots of emotionally charged and ambiguous situations. In *Phoenix* (1999), a series of disjointed, episodic images that appropriate the visual styles of road movies, Westerns, and buddy pictures, two female bounty hunters embark on a manhunt in the American West. In photographs such as *A Lesson for Bobo* (1995), in which two young women, hands defiantly on hips, confront another emerging from a restroom stall, and *Bikini Brawl* (1995), in which one woman is about to strike another with a karate chop, the artist exposes the aggression that lies just below the surface of insecurity and competitiveness. Once again, these images forgo prescribed narratives in order to sharpen their psychological and ideological insights. By representing ambiguous and complex situations rich with nuance, these photographs capture "the coded language of gesture, of the direction of someone's gaze, of the pauses and silences between words that inform and reveal secrets about the ways in which women and girls behave and where they fit in the world."[9]

That men are absent from this imagery, and from the artist's work in general, does not mean they are irrelevant, for the richly encoded communication it represents—the physical signs of rivalry, doubt, ambivalence, or lack of self-confidence—is in many ways motivated by the demands, attention, or inattention of men. This relationship is implied, as well, in *Experiments* wherein a vulnerable "Mother Nature" is imperiled by the negligence and greed of men long empowered to regulate her. It also inspired a political movement with great relevance to Hoey's project: ecological feminism. Born in the 1970s, the ideology of eco-feminism was built on the premise that the masculine imperative to dominate and oppress women is coextensive with man's determination to control and exploit the environment.

***Experiments'* feminism is** implied not only by its female-centric content but also by its metaphorical silences—its refusal to dominate the world by imposing on it an overarching narrative. On one level, our experience of reality cannot be separated from the language we perpetually use to name and define it: "Our vision of the *real* is refracted through the prism of language," writes the literary theorist Naomi Schor. "There exists no relationship to the real which is not mediated through the opaque medium of language. The gaze one brings to bear on the *real* is structured like and above all by language."[10] Nevertheless the imperative towards narrative coherence "has always implied a certain masculine prerogative of ordering" and control, a prerogative that some feminist artists react against through aesthetic fragmentation.[11]

This is precisely the choice made by Ursula K. Le Guin in her eco-feminist tale of environmental disaster and rebirth, *Always Coming Home* (1985), a work eerily similar to *Experiments* in both structure and content. Le Guin's fantasy is set in a post-apocalyptic Northern California of the distant future. It centers on the political and cultural awakening of Stone Telling, a woman torn between the violent, warmongering society of a father she never met and her pacifist maternal homeland. In her journey through the two cultures, Stone Telling tries to understand the contradictions and differences of her parent's conflicting worlds—one a wasteful, militarist society ruled by a rigid patriarchy, the other a Utopian culture dominated by women who reject traditional government, divisions of class and gender, territorial expansion, and human domination of the natural environment. Part science-fiction novel, part textbook, and part anthropological notebook, *Always Coming Home* is an experimental collage of poetry, anecdotes, maps, drawings, journal entries, recipes, and other "documents." The work, originally issued with a cassette of music and poetry, affords a lush, polyphonic view of two cultures, one locked into the past and thus doomed to fail, the other forging a new and revolutionary path to survival.

The novel's aesthetic disunity works on multiple levels. It provides critical distance: by breaking up the world into its constituent details, it allows us to see and understand its subject in fresh and oblique ways. It creates a stylistic counterpart to the story of a Utopian society radically deconstructing itself in order to achieve the reordering necessary to "regain ecological balance."[12] It destabilizes expectations about the relative importance of people, events, and things—the meaning of a relatively modest artifact looms large; a seemingly consequential event proves ordinary—and thus brings into question traditional hierarchies of power and control. It challenges the tyrannical tendency of language and storytelling to unify a complex reality into a narrow and delimiting whole. In its disruption of the "order of things" as established by centuries of masculine authority, *Always Coming Home*—like *Experiments in Primitive Living* a quarter century later—envisions a planet taken apart, rethought, reconfigured, and brought into social and environmental equilibrium by a defiant matriarchy.[13]

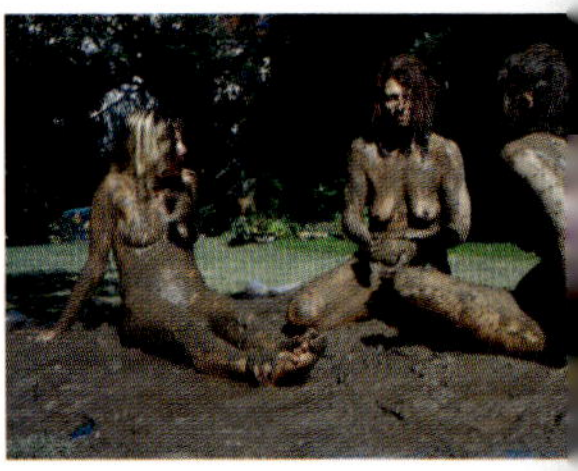

"If a work of art is going to have political resonance, it cannot dictate a story or your experience of it," observes Dana Hoey about her own decidedly matriarchal dismantling of traditional narrative.[14] This deconstruction is evident in serial imagery that seems to tell a lucid story, only to stymie the viewer at every turn. It is evident in a psychologically charged photograph of two bikini-clad young women—*4:03:82* (1995)—an image identified only by time code, as if to emphasize its status as an infinitesimal cut out of a greater, ongoing whole. It is evident in the artist's only time-based work, *One Pro, Two Amateurs* (2000), a video loop of a nude female wrestling match so open-ended that it is almost impossible to discern a beginning or end. These images resonate with the metaphors of silence so central to the feminist and ecological movements. They remind us that what is not said may be more powerful than words, more illuminating than stories.

ENDNOTES

1 Rachel Carson, *Silent Spring* (Boston: Houghton Mifflin, 1962), p. 2

2 Ibid.

3 Jean-François Lyotard, "The Sublime and the Avant-Garde" (1984), in Andrew Benjamin, ed., *The Lyotard Reader* (Hoboken: Wiley-Blackwell, 1991), p. 204

4 Dana Hoey, in conversation with the author, Rheinbeck, New York, 7 June 2009

5 Carson, *Silent Spring*, p. 297

6 Dana Hoey, in Rheinbeck conversation

7 Dana Hoey and Gretchen Rubin, *Profane Waste* (New York: Gregory R. Miller & Co., 2006)

8 Ibid, p. 57

9 Michael O'Sullivan, "Dana Hoey's Blatant Subtlety," *Washington Post* (December 1, 2000), p. N 62

10 Naomi Schor, *Reading in Detail: Aesthetics and the Feminine* (New York and London: Routledge, 2007), p. 103

11 Howard Halle, "New Wave: Four Emerging Photographers," *On Paper* (March/April 1999), p. 34

12 Patrick Murphy, "Voicing Another Nature," in Karen Hohne and Helen Wussow, eds., *A Dialogue of Voices: Feminist Literary Theory and Bakhtin* (Minneapolis: University of Minnesota Press, 1994), p. 77

13 For more on Le Guin's strategies of fragmentation, see ibid, pp. 77–80

14 Dana Hoey, in Rheinbeck conversation

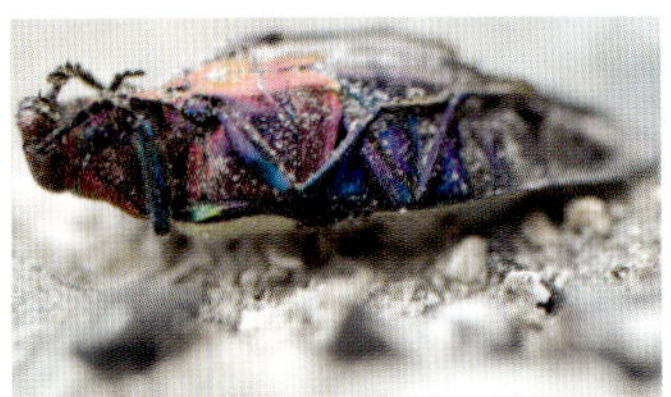

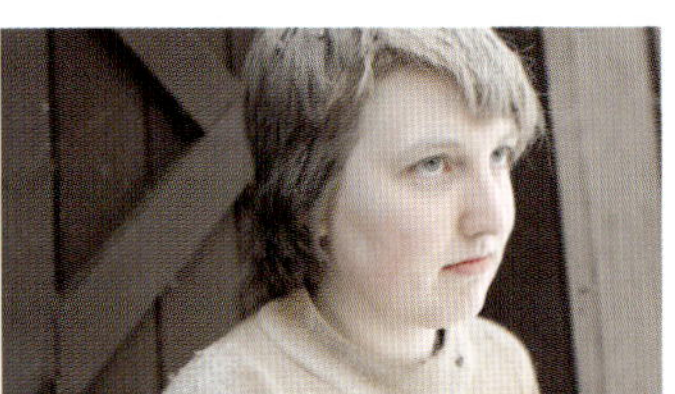

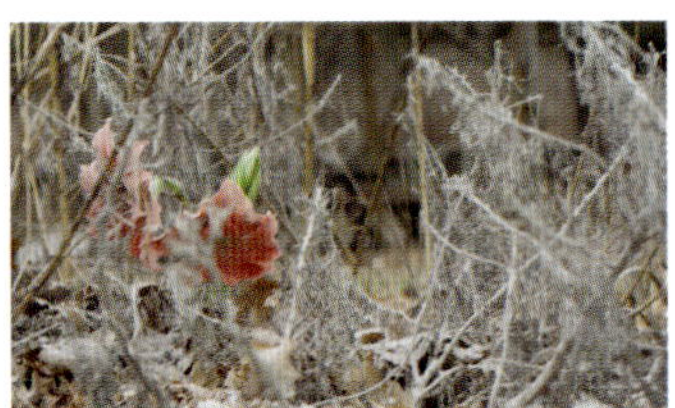

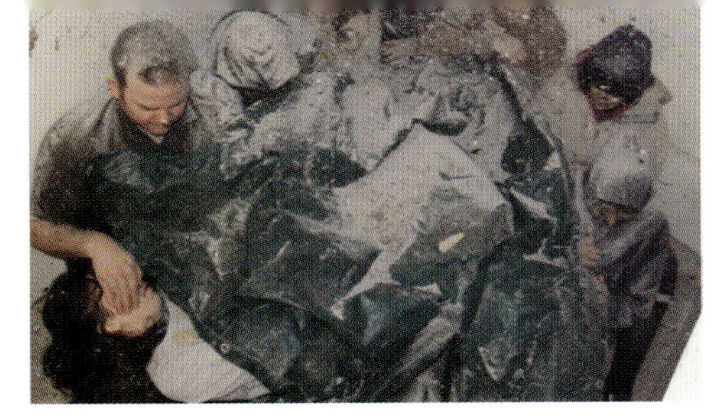

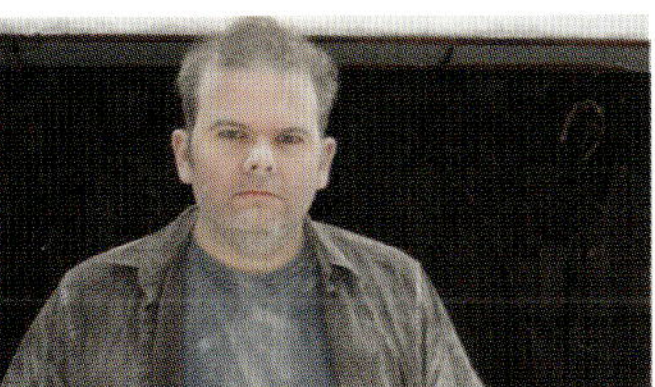

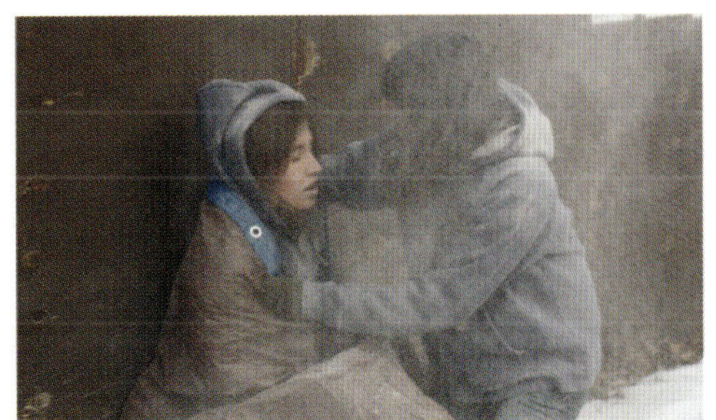

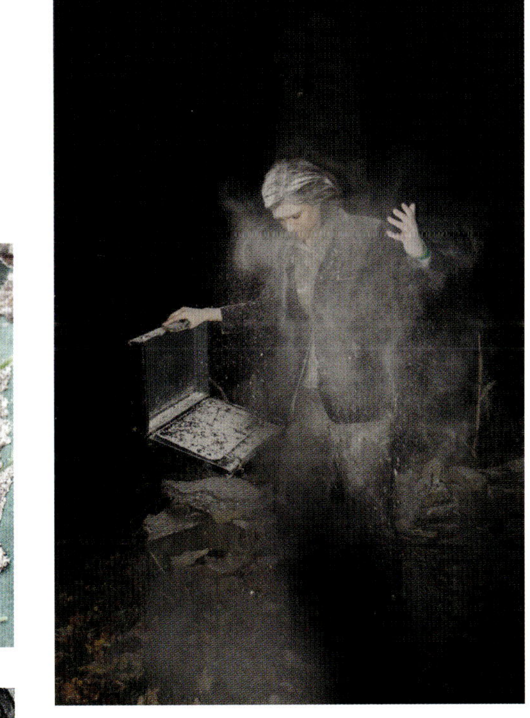

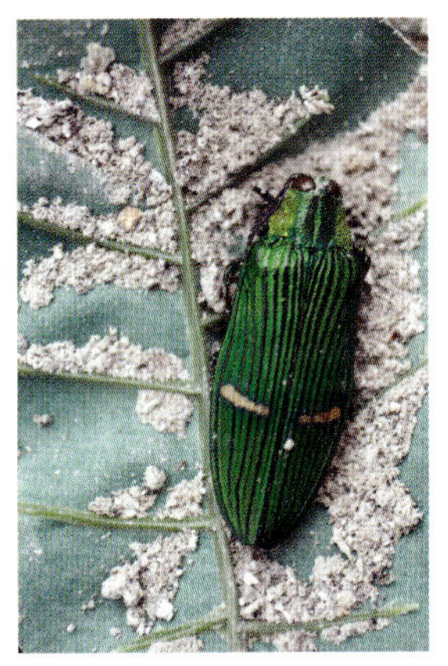

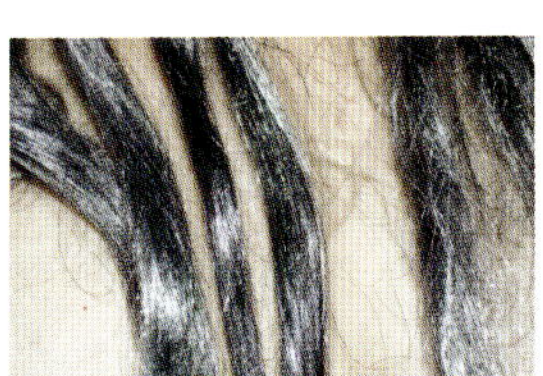

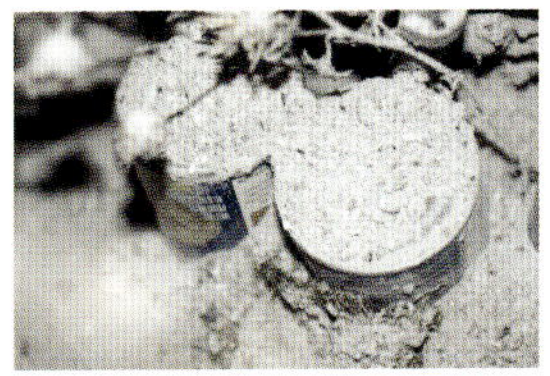

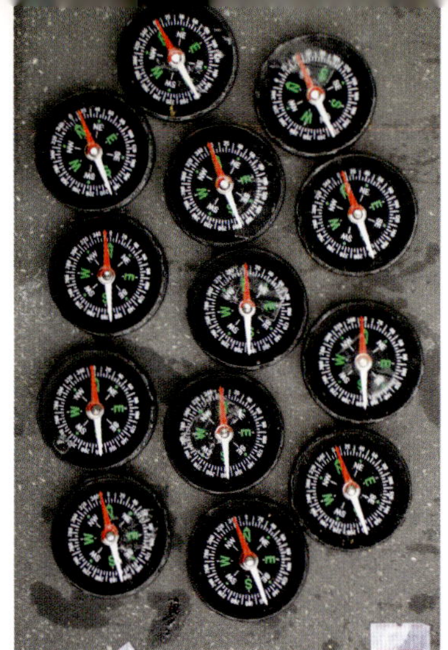

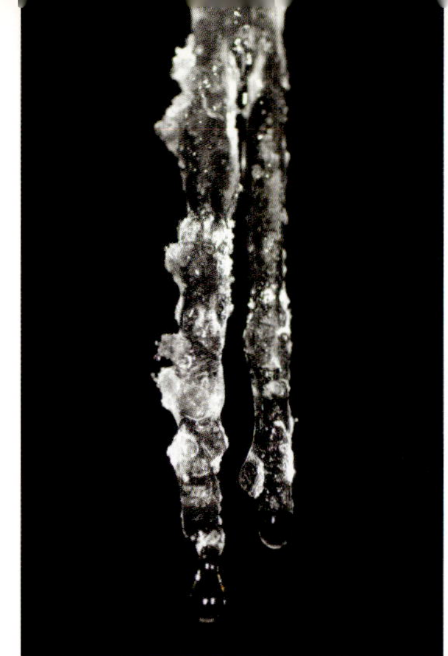

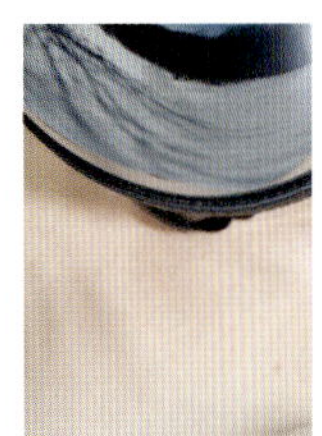

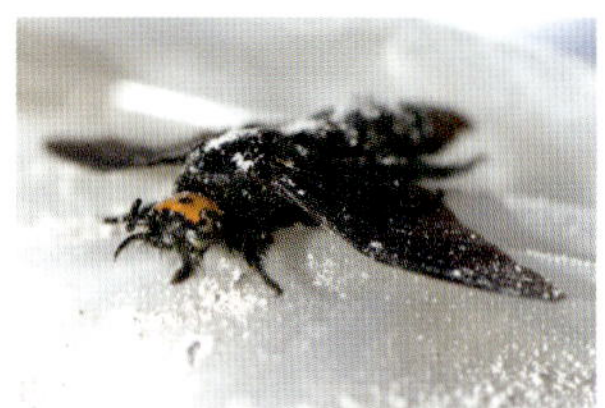

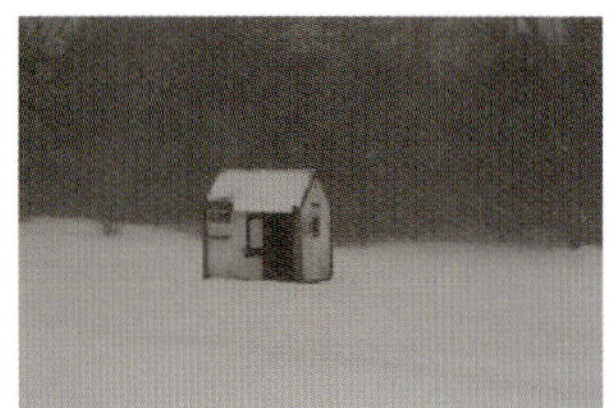

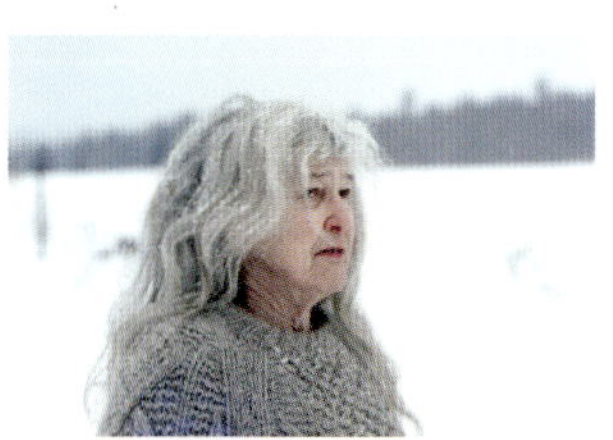

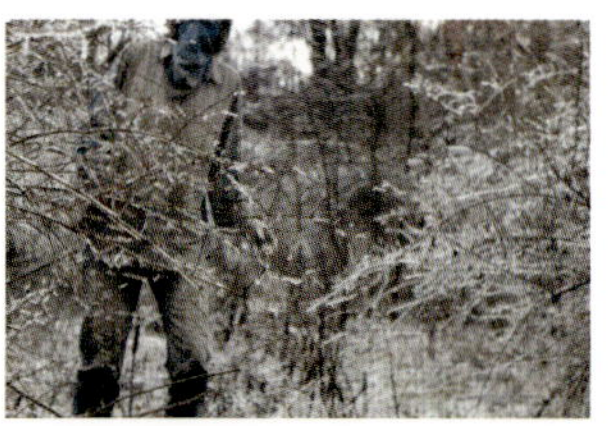

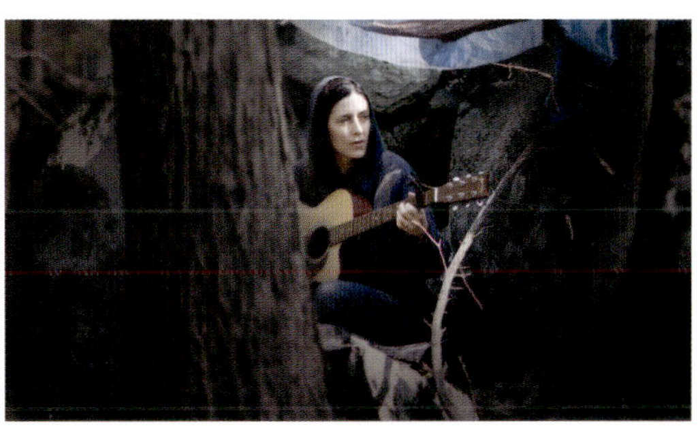

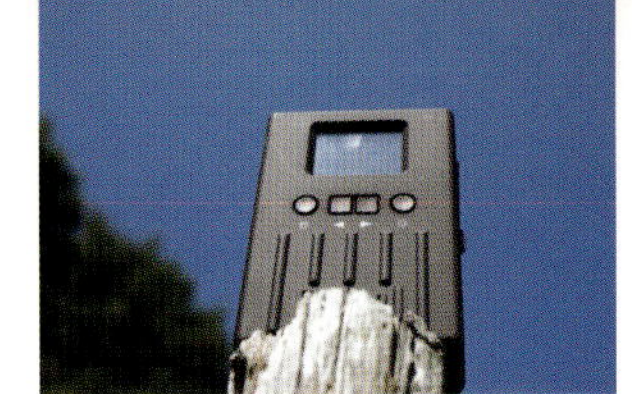

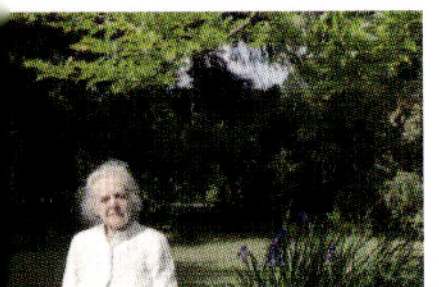

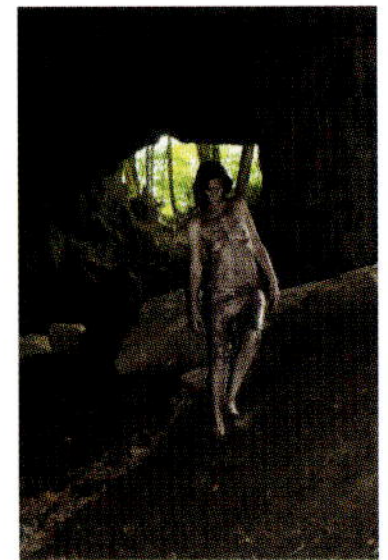

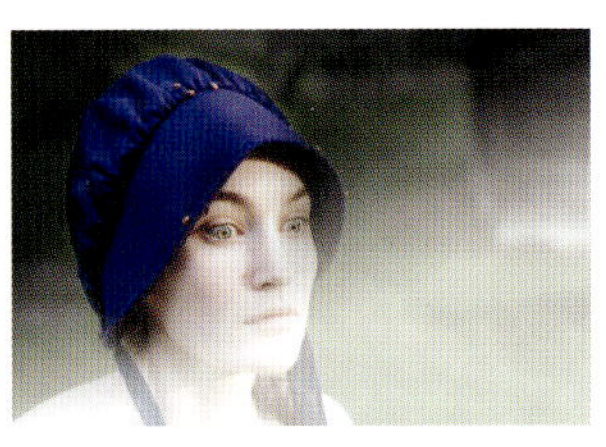

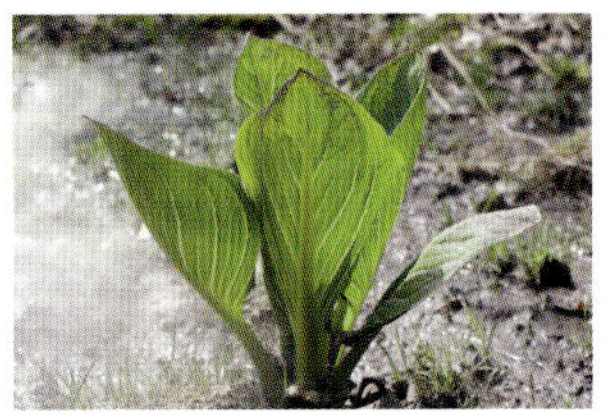

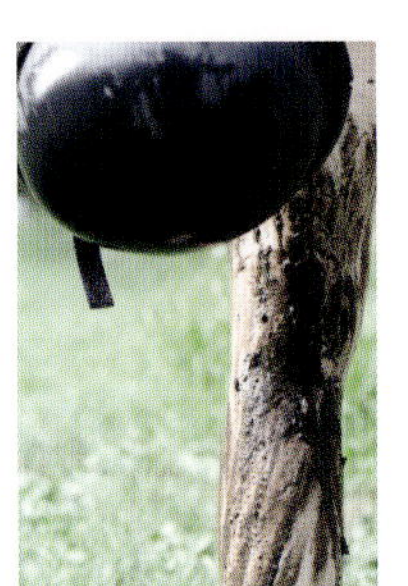

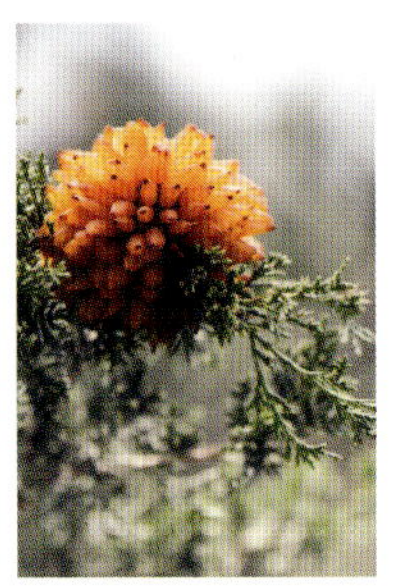

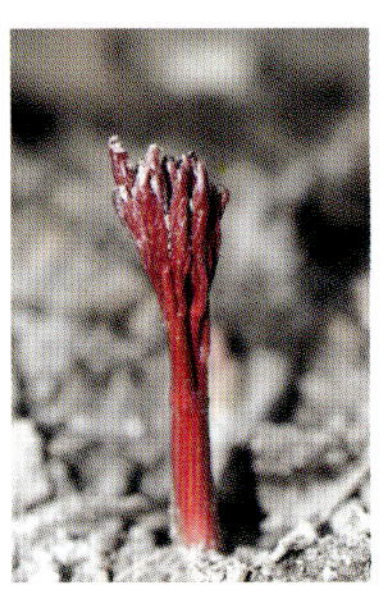

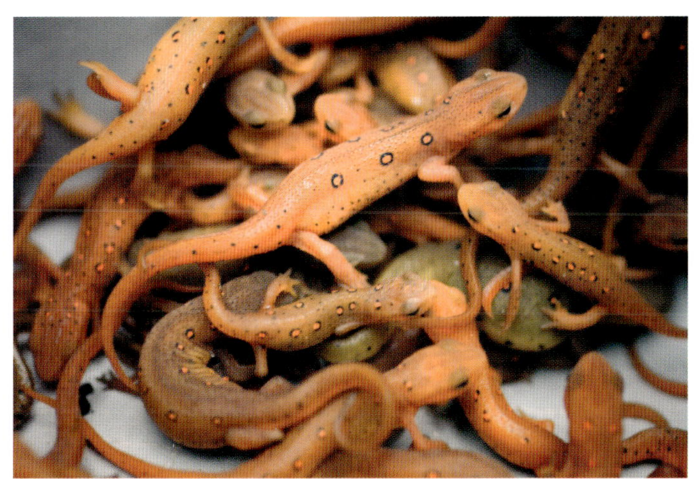

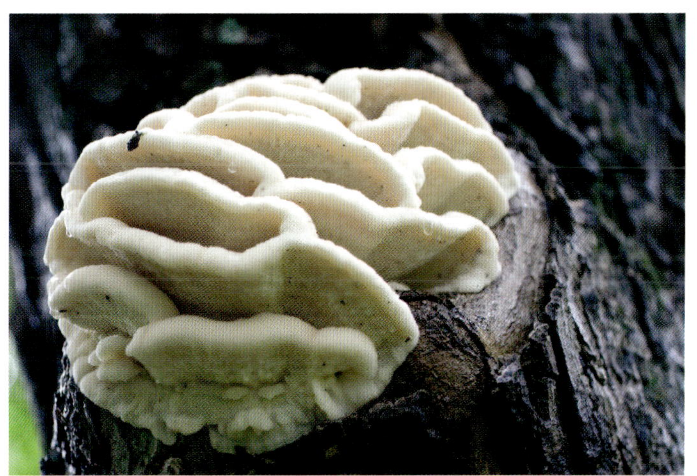

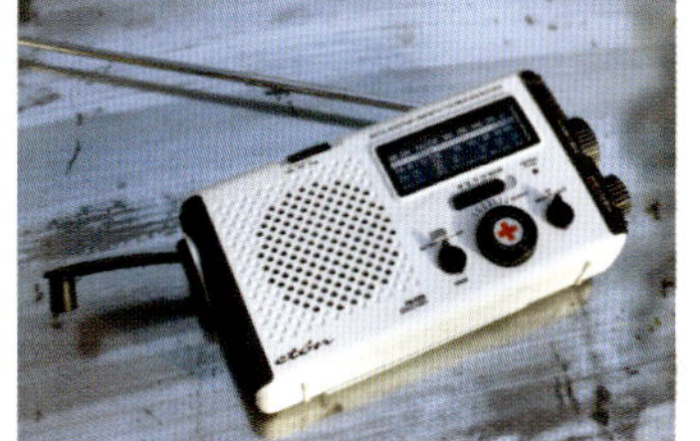

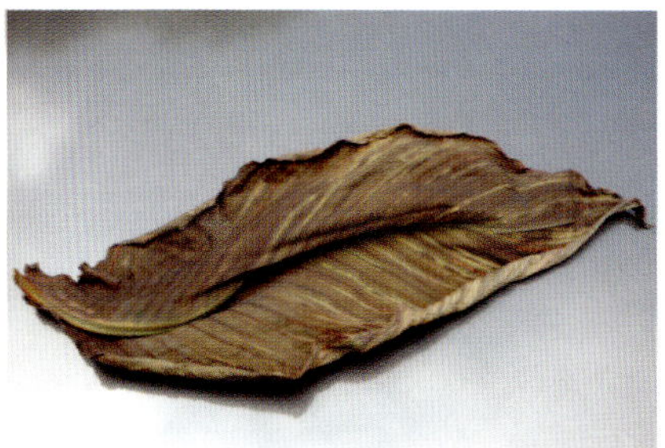

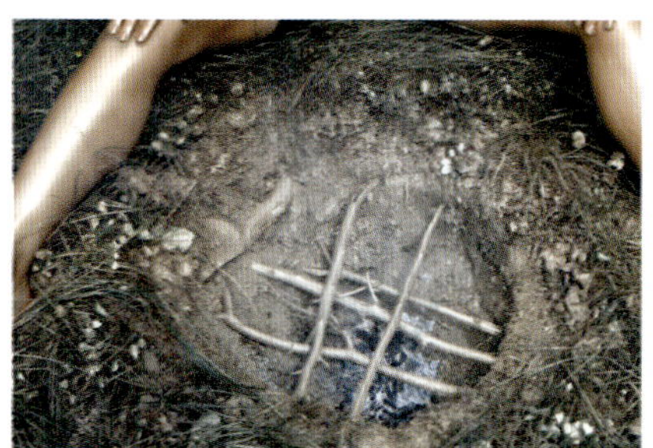

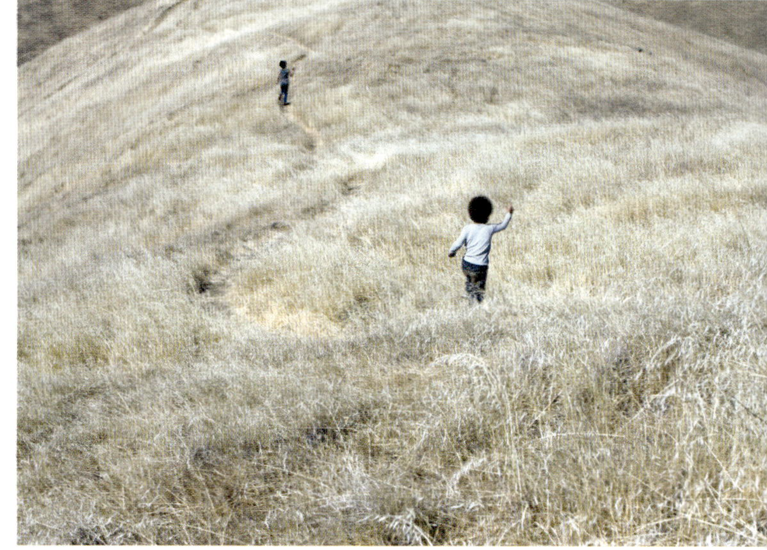

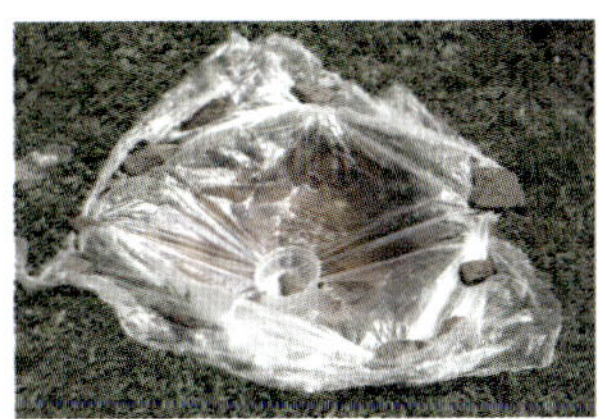

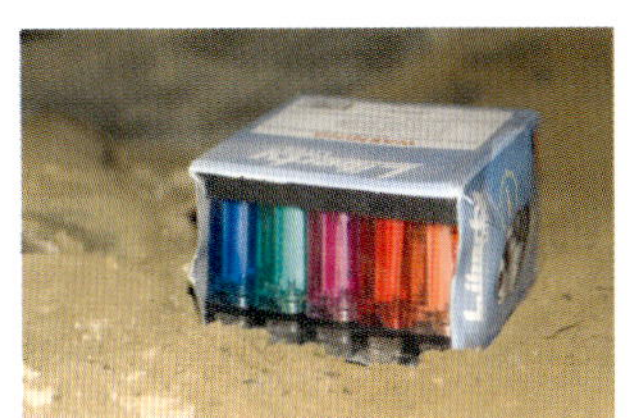

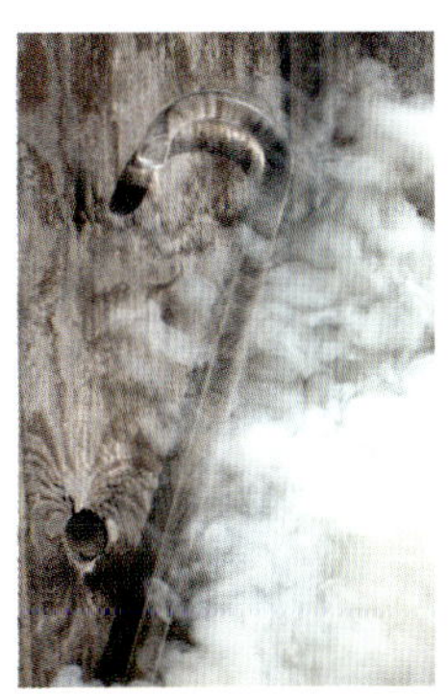

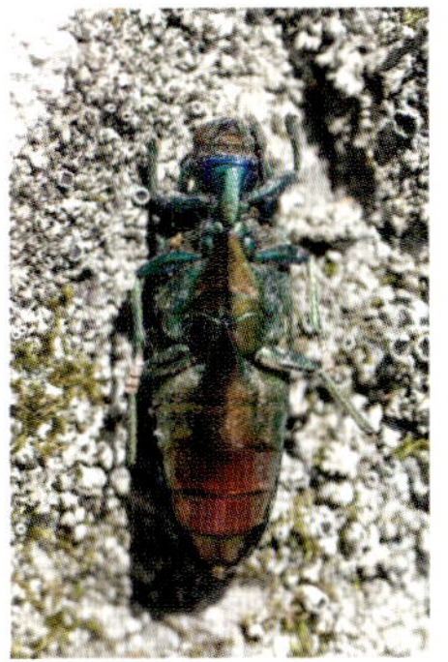

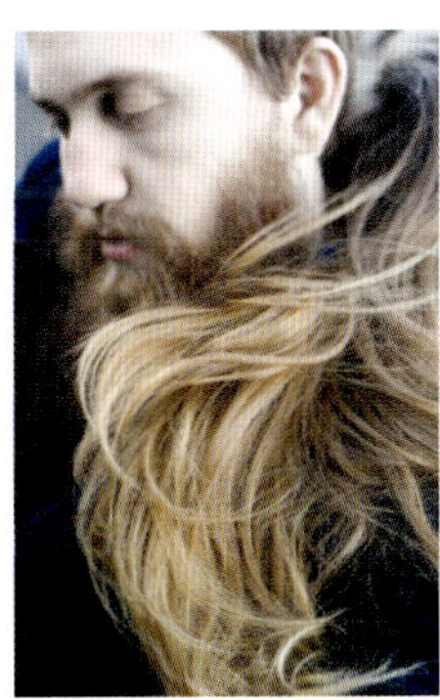

EXPERIMENTS IN PRIMITIVE LIVING

Archival inkjet prints/edition 1/5 + 1 artist proof/dimensions: framed
Courtesy of the artist and the Friedrich Petzel Gallery, New York

ASH

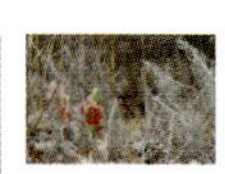

AMARYLLIS
2007
19 ¾ x 27 ¾ inches

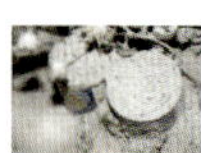

CANS
2007
19 ¾ x 27 ¾ inches

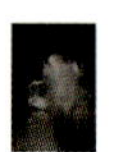

DOUBLE CHECK
2007
64 ¾ x 44 ¾ inches

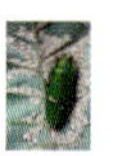

GREEN BUG
2007
27 ¾ x 19 ¾ inches

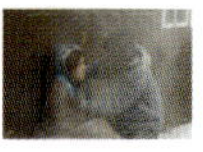

JO
2008
19 ¾ x 27 ¾ inches

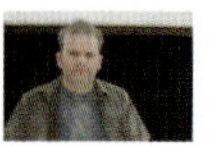

KAI
2008
19 ¾ x 27 ¾ inches

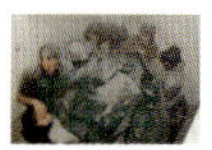

MENTOR GROUP
2008
24 ¾ x 34 ¾ inches

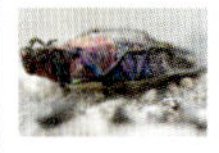

RAINBOW BUG
2008
19 ¾ x 27 ¾ inches

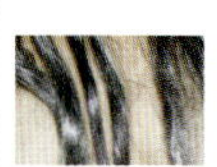

THE POLICE
2008
19 ¾ x 27 ¾ inches

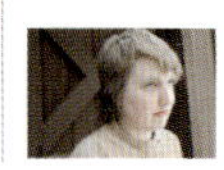

ZOE
2008
19 ¾ x 27 ¾ inches

FREEZE

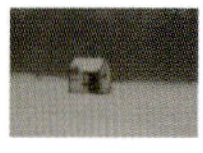

BIRD HOUSE
2006
13 ¾ x 18 ¾ inches

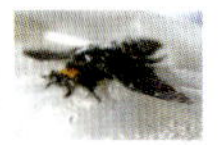

BLACK BUG
2006
13 ¾ x 18 ¾ inches

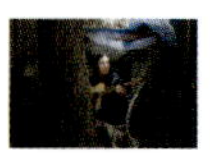

BLIND GUITAR PLAYER
2008
19 ¾ x 22 ¾ inches

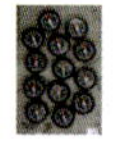

COMPASSES
2008
18 ¾ x 13 ¾ inches

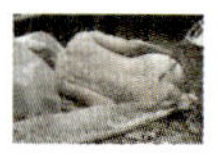

FALLEN
2007
19 ¾ x 27 ¾ inches

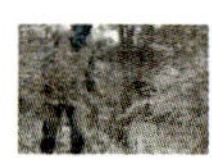

ICE STORM
2008
24 ¾ x 34 ¾ inches

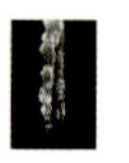

ICICLES
2008
27 ¾ x 19 ¾ inches

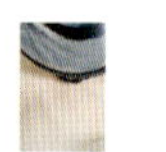

HELMET
2007
27 ¾ x 19 ¾ inchess

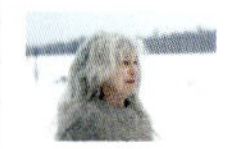

RANDY
2005
19 ¾ x 27 ¾ inches

THAW

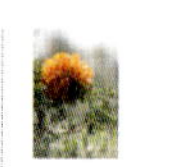

CEDAR RUST
2008
27 ¾ x 19 ¾ inches

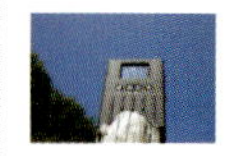

GAME CAMERA
2008
13 ¾ x 18 ¾ inches

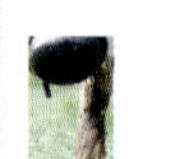

HELMET
2006
27 ¾ x 19 ¾ inches

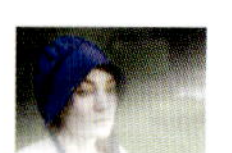

JULIA
2006
19 ¾ x 27 ¾ inches

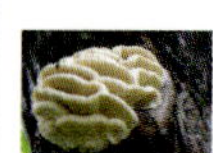

MAPLE FUNGUS
2008
19 ¾ x 27 ¾ inches

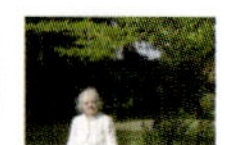

MRS. JACOBY
2005
19 ¾ x 27 ¾ inches

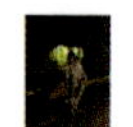

OIL CAVE
2008
18 ¾ x 13 ¾ inches

PROFANE WASTE

Archival inkjet prints/edition 1/5 + 1 artist proof/dimensions: framed
Courtesy of the artist and the Friedrich Petzel Gallery, New York

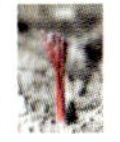

PEONY
2008
34 ¾ x 24 ¾ inches

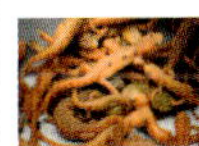

SALAMANDERS
2008
19 ¾ x 27 ¾ inches

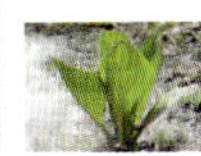

SKUNK CABBAGE
2008
19 ¾ x 27 ¾ inches

FLOOD

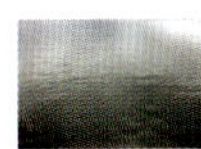

FLOOD
2008
44 ¾ x 64 ¾ inches

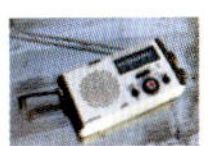

RADIO
2008
13 ¾ x 18 ¾ inches

DROUGHT

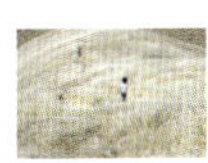

AYLER
2008
44 ¾ x 64 ¾ inches

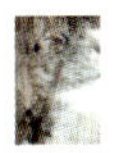

CANE
2008
27 ¾ x 19 ¾ inches

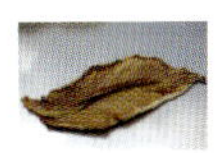

CANNA
2008
13 ¾ x 18 ¾ inches

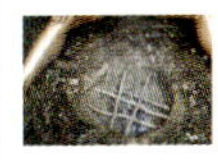

DAKOTA FIREPIT
2008
19 ¾ x 27 ¾ inches

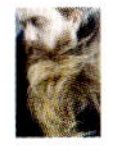

FEMALE MAN
2008
27 ¾ x 19 ¾ inches

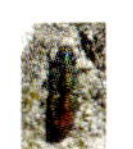

DRY BUG
2007
27 ¾ x 27 ¾ inches

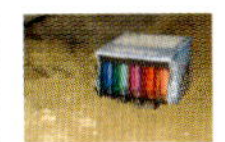

LIGHTERS
2008
19 ¾ x 27 ¾ inches

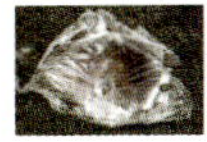

SOLAR STILL
2008
19 ¾ x 27 ¾ inches

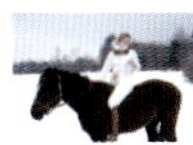

PREGNANT SMOKER 2
2001
16 ¾ x 23 ¼ inches

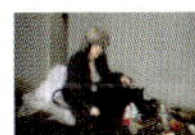

SPENT OUT
2005
16 ¾ x 23 ¼ inches

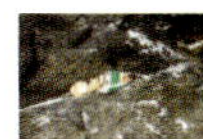

POPE SALT SACRIFICE
2005
16 ¾ x 23 ¼ inches

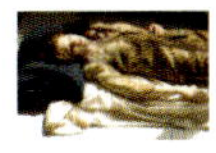

YOUNG PAINTER
2005
16 ¾ x 23 ¼ inches

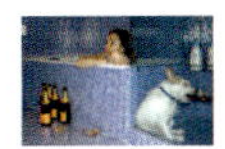

CHAMPAGNE BATH
2005
16 ¾ x 23 ¼ inches

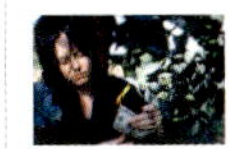

PROFANE WASTE
2001
49 x 39 ¼ inches

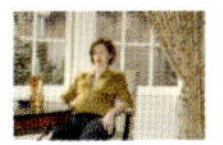

DEWAR'S MOTHER
2005
16 ¾ x 23 ¼ inches

ONE PRO, TWO AMATEURS

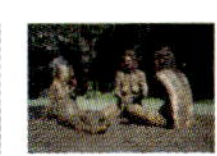

Color DVD
10 minutes, 16 seconds

Courtesy of the artist and the Friedrich Petzel Gallery

DANA HOEY

Born in 1966, San Francisco, California
Lives and works in New York

EDUCATION

1997	Yale University, MFA, Photography
1989	Wesleyan University, BA, Philosophy

SOLO EXHIBITIONS

2010	*Experiments in Primitive Living*. Center for Art, Design and Visual Culture, University of Maryland Baltimore County. Curated by Maurice Berger
2008	Friedrich Petzel Gallery, New York
2006	*Pattern Recognition*. Friedrich Petzel Gallery, New York
2002	*Moon Bitches*. Friedrich Petzel Gallery, New York
2001	*Dana Hoey*. Tache-Levy, Brussels
2000	*Dana Hoey*. Hirshhorn Museum and Sculpture Garden, Washington, D.C.
1999	*Phoenix*. Friedrich Petzel Gallery, New York
1997	*Dana Hoey*. Friedrich Petzel Gallery, New York

GROUP EXHIBITIONS

2009	*Born in the morning, dead by night*. Leo Koenig, Inc., New York. Curated by Tony Matelli
2008	*The Human Face is a Monument*. Guild & Greyshkul, New York
2007	*People Take Pictures of Each Other*. LaMontagne Gallery, Boston. Curated by Bob Nickas
	The Lath Picture Show. Friedrich Petzel Gallery, New York
	For the People of Paris. Sutton Lane, Paris
2006	*COMPLICIT! Contemporary American Art and Mass Culture*. University of Virginia Art Museum, Charlottesville
2005	*Focus On: New Photography*. Norton Museum of Art, West Palm Beach
2004	*American Stars 'N Bars*. Guggenheim Gallery, Chapman University, Orange, CA
	The Amazing and the Immutable. University of South Florida Contemporary Art, Tufts University Art Gallery, Boston
2003	*Girls on Film*. Produce Gallery, Penrose Gallery, Tyler School of Art, Temple University, Philadelphia. Curated by Joseph R. Wolin
	Faking Real. Le Roy Neiman Gallery, Columbia University, New York

2002 *Portrait as Performance*. Hand Workshop Art Center, Richmond; Contemporary Art Center of Virginia, Virginia Beach

Art Downtown: New Photography. Wall Street Rising, New York. Curated by Richard Marshall

2001 *Driving Women*. The Castle Gallery, The College of New Rochelle

Dana Hoey, Tom Hunter, Adam Baer. 51 Fine Art Photography, Antwerp

Oliver Boberg, Dana Hoey, Cadida Hofer, Vic Muniz & Sarah Rossiter. G Fine Art, Washington, D.C.

2000 *Shivers*. Cesare Manzo Gallery, Pescara

And she will have your eyes... Galerie Analix Forever, Geneva

Charline von Heyl & Dana Hoey. Friedrich Petzel Gallery, New York

One Night Stand. Joao Ferreira Fine Art, Cape Town. Curated by Amanda Williamson and Justine Wheeler

Girlfriend. Galerie fur Zeitgenössische Kunst Leipzig. Curated by Sarah Morris

Potent/Present: Selections from the Vicki and Kent Logan Collection. California College of Arts and Crafts, Oakland (cat.)

Fact/Fiction: Contemporary Art That Walks the Line. San Francisco Museum of Modern Art

The New Generation of American Photographers. Kohn Turner Gallery, Los Angeles; Gallery 312, Chicago. Organized by *Harper's Bazaar*

Greater New York. P.S.1, New York (cat.)

Innuendo. Dee Glasoe, New York. Curated by Doug Wada

1999 *Mr. Fascination*. Thread Waxing Space, New York. Curated by Lia Gangitano

Salome: Images of Women in Contemporary Art. The Castle Gallery, The College of New Rochelle, New York. Curated by Katherine Gass. (cat.)

Uncanny. Fotomuseum Winterthur (cat.)

Another Girl, Another Planet. Greenberg Van Doren Fine Art, New York. Curated by Gregory Crewdson and Jeanne Greenberg, Lawrence Rubin

art lovers. The Liverpool Biennial of Contemporary Art (cat.) Curated by Marcia Fortes

1998 *Color*. Edwynn Houk Gallery, New York

Some Young New Yorkers II. P.S.1, New York. Curated by Alanna Heiss and Klaus Biesenbach

X-Change. Gisela Capitain Gallery, Cologne. With Jenny Gage and Anna Gaskell

1997 *Graduate Photography at Yale.* Yale University School of Art (cat.)

High Anxiety. Miami-Dade Community College, Florida

The Name of the Place. Casey Kaplan Gallery, New York. Curated by Laurie Simmons

New Photography. David Klein Gallery, Birmingham

1996 *a/drift.* Center for Curatorial Studies Museum, Bard College, Annandale-on-Hudson, New York. Curated by Joshua Decter

Making Pictures: Women and Photography 1975-Now. Nicole Klagsbrun Gallery, New York. Traveled to Bernard Toale Gallery, Boston

Sugar Mountain. White Columns, New York. Curated by Andrea Scott and Paul Ha

Summer Group Show. Friedrich Petzel Gallery, New York

High Anxiety. Woodstock Center of Photography, Woodstock. Curated by Joe Wolin

Blur vs Oasis. New York. Curated by Bill Arning

PUBLIC COLLECTIONS

Hirshhorn Museum and Sculpture Garden, Smithsonian Institution

Los Angeles Museum of Contemporary Art

Middlebury College Museum of Art

National Museum of Women in the Arts, Washington, D.C.

Norton Museum of Art

San Francisco Museum of Modern Art

Solomon R. Guggenheim Museum, New York

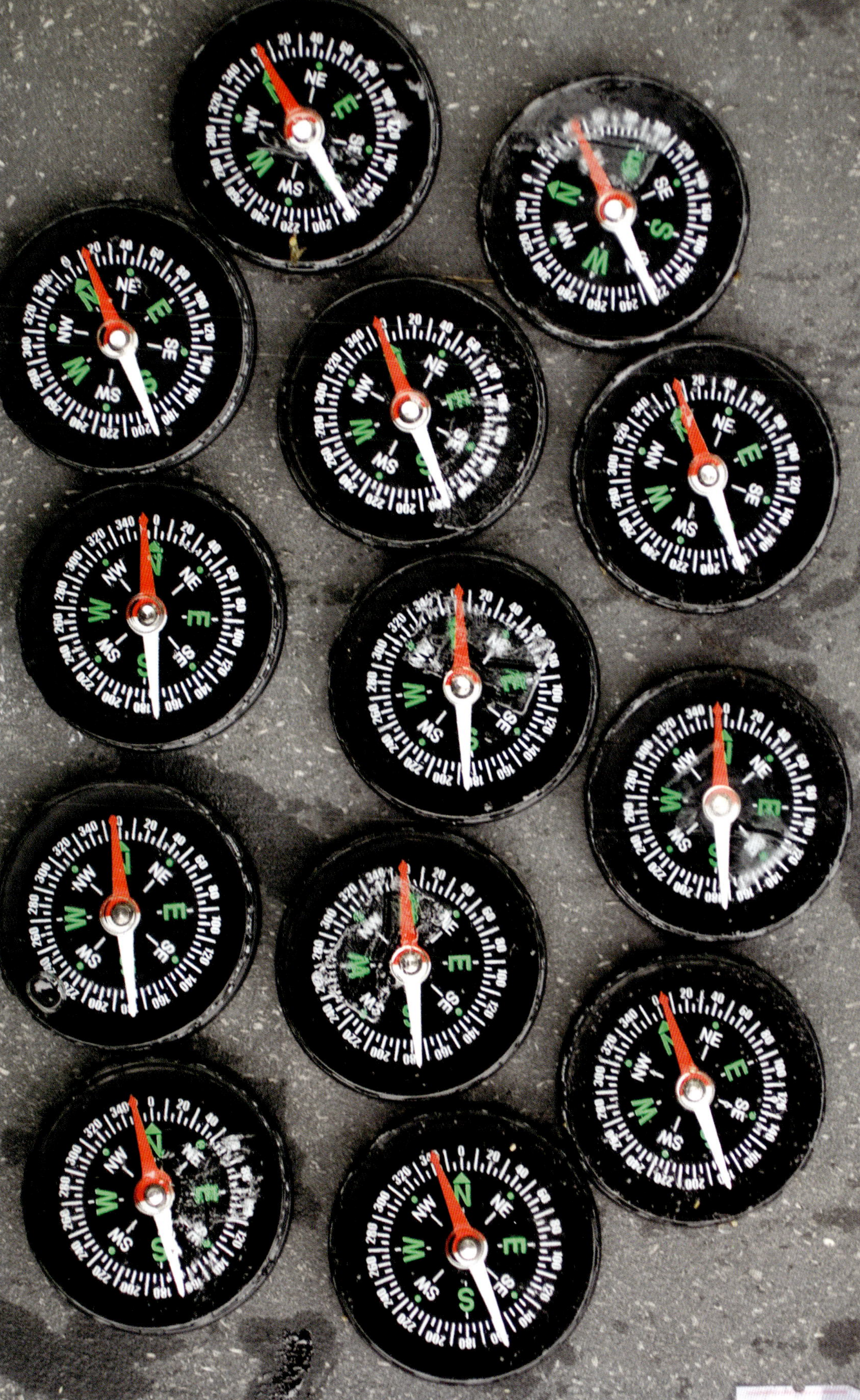

Center for Art, Design and Visual Culture

Published by the Center for Art, Design and Visual Culture
University of Maryland Baltimore County
Baltimore, Maryland 21250

www.umbc.edu/cadvc

Library of Congress Control Number 2009937727
ISSN 15211223

ISBN 978-1-890761-13-4

design and typography by guenet abraham